SO-BBT-059

THE EMANCIPATION PROCLAMATION

BY G. S. PRENTZAS

CHILDREN'S PRESS®

An Imprint of Scholastic Inc.

New York Toronto London Auckland Sydney
Mexico City New Delhi Hong Kong
Danbury, Connecticut

BRINGING HISTORY to LIFE

Content Consultant
James Marten, PhD
Professor and Chair, History Department
Marquette University
Milwaukee, Wisconsin

Library of Congress Cataloging-in-Publication Data
Prentzas, G. S.
  The Emancipation Proclamation/by G. S. Prentzas.
     p. cm.—(Cornerstones of freedom)
  Includes bibliographical references and index.
  ISBN-13: 978-0-531-25032-7 (lib. bdg.)   ISBN-10: 0-531-25032-6 (lib. bdg.)
  ISBN-13: 978-0-531-26557-4 (pbk.)   ISBN-10: 0-531-26557-9 (pbk.)
  1. United States. President (1861–1865 : Lincoln). Emancipation
Proclamation—Juvenile literature. 2. Lincoln, Abraham,
1809–1865—Juvenile literature. 3. Slaves—Emancipation—United
States—Juvenile literature. 4. United States—Politics and
Government—1861–1865—Juvenile literature. I. Title.
  E453.P85 2012
  973.7'14—dc22   2011011969

1 2 3 4 5 6 7 8 9 10 R 21 20 19 18 17 16 15 14 13 12

Photographs © 2012: AP Images: 36; G.S. Prentzas: 64; Library of
Congress: 21 (Brady-Handy Photograph Collection), 4 bottom, 4 top, 23,
24 (Alexander Gardner), 29 (Hoxie Collection), 27 (Timothy H. O'Sullivan),
5 bottom, 39 (W. Roberts/R.A. Dimmick), 13 (Andrew J. Russell), cover, 22;
National Archives and Records Administration: 14; North Wind Picture
Archives: 18, 50; ShutterStock, Inc.: 54 (George Pappas), back cover
(Cedric Weber); The Granger Collection, New York: 38, 56 bottom (Mathew
Brady Studio), 19 (Alonzo Chappel), 41 (Currier & Ives), 16 (Benjamin
Robert Haydon), 2, 3, 12 (Theodor Kaufmann), 5 top, 47, 59 (Kurz & Allison),
33 (Thomas Satterwhite Noble), 6, 8, 10, 11, 20, 26, 30, 31, 34, 37, 40, 42, 44,
46, 48, 56 top, 57, 58.

Did you know that studying history can be fun?

BRING HISTORY TO LIFE by becoming a history investigator. Examine the evidence (primary and secondary source materials); cross-examine the people and witnesses. Take a look at what was happening at the time—but be careful! What happened years ago might suddenly become incredibly interesting and change the way you think!

Contents

Slavery in America

Slaves were often sold at auctions.

European colonists who settled in North America began importing black slaves from Africa in 1619. Most slaves worked as laborers on Southern plantations. They grew crops such as cotton and tobacco. Other enslaved people worked as servants in their masters' homes. The South's economy came to depend heavily on slave labor.

Yet the question of slavery was a hotly debated issue between pro-slavery and antislavery groups. Eight Northern states had outlawed slavery by 1804. Several nearby countries abolished slavery completely. Mexico outlawed it in 1810. By the late 1850s, Cuba, Brazil, and the United States were the only three places in the Americas where slavery was still legal. Historian John Hope Franklin observed, "The United States, the leader in political independence, was lagging far behind in the cause of human freedom."

About four million people of African descent were enslaved in the United States by 1860. **Abolitionists** encouraged people to free their slaves. Many people also believed that the U.S. Congress should prevent slavery in new western territories that the nation had acquired. But most Southerners believed that each state should have the right to determine if it wanted to allow slavery.

The opposing beliefs about the practice slowly split the nation in two. This eventually caused the North and South to take up arms against each other in the American Civil War. The issues of slavery and states' rights nearly tore the country apart.

POPULATION WAS ENSLAVED PEOPLE.

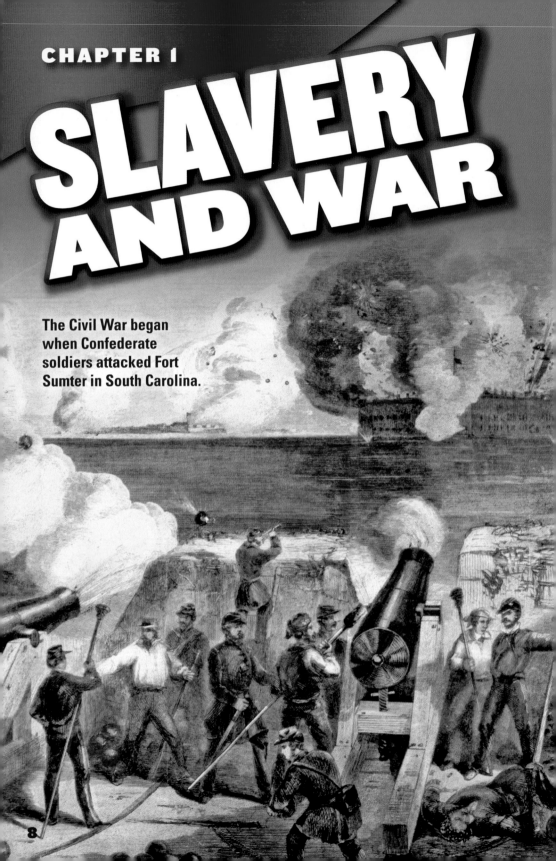

CHAPTER 1

SLAVERY AND WAR

The Civil War began when Confederate soldiers attacked Fort Sumter in South Carolina.

THE CIVIL WAR BEGAN IN April 1861. The United States was called the Union. It had many advantages over the 11 states in the newly formed Confederate States of America, or Confederacy. The Union had about five times as many factories as the Confederacy did. Its network of railroads included twice as many miles of tracks. Its banks had four times the amount of money.

The North's major crops were corn, wheat, and oats. The South's were cotton, tobacco, and rice. Only the rice could feed Confederate troops. The Union army was better equipped. It also had more than two million soldiers. This made it twice the size of the Confederate army.

These disadvantages did not keep the Confederacy from winning most of the battles in the first year of the war. Many citizens and politicians in the North questioned whether President Abraham Lincoln could lead the Union to victory.

Lincoln became the 16th president of the United States in 1861.

A President's Dilemma

Lincoln had promised during his 1860 presidential campaign to prevent slavery from expanding into the country's western territories. He personally opposed slavery. But he also recognized the legal and political difficulties of abolishing it entirely. Lincoln declared at his **inauguration** in March 1861 that he did not intend to interfere with slavery in the South. He avoided taking action to end slavery during his first year in office. He claimed that the only objective of the war was to preserve the Union.

Lincoln feared that **emancipating** the slaves would cause the border states of Delaware, Maryland, Kentucky, and Missouri to join the Confederacy. Slavery was still legal in these four states. Losing them might give the Confederacy the upper hand in the war. Lincoln also worried that many Union soldiers would refuse to fight if the war became viewed as an effort to free slaves rather than to reunite the country.

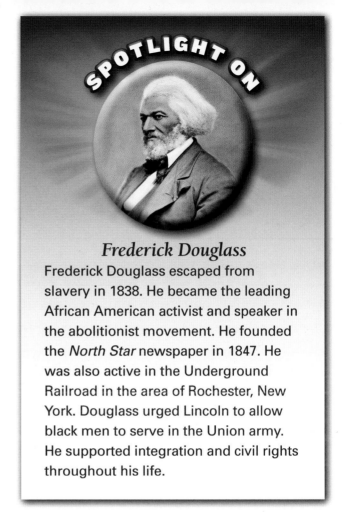

Frederick Douglass

Frederick Douglass escaped from slavery in 1838. He became the leading African American activist and speaker in the abolitionist movement. He founded the *North Star* newspaper in 1847. He was also active in the Underground Railroad in the area of Rochester, New York. Douglass urged Lincoln to allow black men to serve in the Union army. He supported integration and civil rights throughout his life.

Legal Issues

Few people viewed slavery as the reason for the conflict at first. Southern states claimed that they had **seceded** from the Union because the federal government interfered with their rights. Northerners felt that states could not secede from the Union. Henry Ward Beecher, Frederick Douglass, and other leading abolitionists began pressuring Lincoln to end slavery.

But Lincoln believed that the U.S. Constitution did not give the president or Congress the power to prevent a state legislature from making slavery legal within its own borders. Lincoln believed that he could not seize a citizen's property, including slaves, without **due process** of the law.

Congress Takes Action

Congress tried to make it clear in July 1861 that ending slavery was not the objective of the war. It passed a **resolution** stating that the war was being fought to defend the Constitution and to preserve the Union.

Many escaped slaves fled to Northern states, where they were less likely to be captured.

Under the Confiscation Act, escaped Southern slaves worked at jobs such as building railroads in the North.

Lincoln had ordered his military commanders not to allow black men to join the Union army. But Confederate leaders allowed slaves to work in factories and do other war-related jobs.

Congress passed the Confiscation Act in August. This was the first of several laws that took away a slaveholder's ownership rights to any slave who engaged in military activity against the United States. Many Union commanders had returned runaway slaves to their owners before the act was passed. The first Confiscation Act said that runaway slaves were **contraband**. U.S. commanders could now take in slaves fleeing the South and put them to work for the Union army. But black men still could not serve as soldiers.

A FIRSTHAND LOOK AT
THE DISTRICT OF COLUMBIA EMANCIPATION ACT

Abraham Lincoln signed the District of Columbia Emancipation Act on April 16, 1862. It immediately freed about 3,000 slaves in the nation's capital. It also signaled that the federal government was taking action against the institution of slavery. The act set up a board that approved requests from slave owners who wanted to be compensated for losing their slaves. See page 60 for links to view the original document and a version of the complete text online.

A FIRSTHAND LOOK AT

PRESIDENT LINCOLN'S RESPONSE TO GENERAL ORDER NO. 11

On May 9, 1862, Union general David Hunter issued General Order No. 11 from his headquarters on Hilton Head Island, South Carolina. It ordered that all slaves in Georgia, Florida, and South Carolina were "forever free." See page 60 for a link to view Lincoln's original handwritten reversal of Hunter's order.

Congress passed a law in April 1862 that freed all slaves in the District of Columbia. The legislation provided a fund of $1 million to **compensate** slave owners for the loss of their slaves. Congress passed another law two months later abolishing slavery in the nation's vast western territories. It provided no compensation for slave owners.

Military Necessity

Some Union commanders believed that the slaves should be freed and allowed to fight against the Confederates. General David Hunter took action. He led the Union forces that captured Fort Pulaski near Savannah, Georgia, in May 1862. Hunter issued a military order freeing all of the slaves in Georgia, Florida, and South Carolina. Lincoln quickly reversed Hunter's order. He asserted that only the president had the power to issue a wartime order freeing slaves.

CHAPTER 2

LINCOLN'S DECISION

The issue of slavery was debated even outside of the United States. Here, a group of abolitionists hold a meeting in London, England.

ABOLITIONISTS, POLITICIANS, and many religious groups continued to pressure Lincoln to make a decision on the issue of slavery. The number of slaves escaping to the safety of the Union army increased as the war progressed. Large camps of slaves sprung up around Union military posts.

Lincoln continued to avoid making public statements about his position on freeing slaves. But he had already decided to issue an emancipation order. He had become increasingly concerned about the Confederacy's use of slaves in its war effort. Slave labor improved the Confederates' ability to wage war. Freeing slaves would help reduce that advantage.

Lincoln chose his words carefully when drafting the Emancipation Proclamation.

Drafting the Proclamation

Lincoln began writing the Emancipation **Proclamation** in June 1862. He often worked in the quiet surroundings of the War Department telegraph office. Lincoln showed the first draft of the proclamation to Vice President Hannibal Hamlin on June 18. The vice president suggested a few minor changes. Lincoln edited the proclamation. He then showed the draft to two of his closest advisers, Secretary of State William H. Seward and Secretary of the Navy Gideon Welles. They also suggested changes.

Major Thomas T. Eckert was the officer in charge of the War Department telegraph office. He later provided an eyewitness account of Lincoln at work composing the Emancipation Proclamation. Eckert wrote that the president "would look out of the window a while and then put his pen to paper, but he did not write much at once. . . . [W]hen he had made up his mind he would put down a line or two, and then sit quiet for a few minutes." See page 60 for a link to view Eckert's account online.

Informing the Cabinet

Lincoln called together all the secretaries of the seven executive branch departments on July 22. This group of department heads has traditionally been called the president's cabinet. He told the men that he had decided to issue an order that would free the slaves.

Lincoln's cabinet considered the potential outcome of the proclamation.

Montgomery Blair pointed out the political consequences that the proclamation was likely to have.

Several cabinet members supported the decision. Treasury Secretary Salmon Chase suggested that freed slaves be allowed to join the Union army. Postmaster General Montgomery Blair worried that Lincoln's order would lead to the loss of Republican Party congressional seats in the coming fall elections. Lincoln was a Republican. He would have more trouble conducting the war if Democrats held the majority in Congress.

Secretary of War Edwin Stanton questioned the timing of the order. The Union army was still losing battles in the East. Many citizens remained highly critical of the way Lincoln was conducting the war. Stanton suggested that Lincoln wait to issue the proclamation "until you can give it to the country supported by military success." Lincoln and the other cabinet members agreed with Stanton's reasoning.

Waiting

Horace Greeley was the editor of the *New York Tribune*. He published an open letter to Lincoln in his newspaper on August 20, 1862. He criticized the president for avoiding the issue of slavery. Greeley had

Edwin Stanton's input encouraged Lincoln to wait to release the proclamation until the Union army had gained the upper hand in the war.

a great influence on public opinion. Lincoln could not ignore the comments. He responded by writing, "My paramount object in this struggle is to save the Union, and is not either to save or to destroy slavery." Lincoln had already decided to free the slaves. But he did not want to reveal his plans at that time.

Lincoln continued to wait through the summer for the Union victory he urgently needed. On

YESTERDAY'S HEADLINES

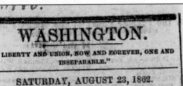

WASHINGTON.
"LIBERTY AND UNION, NOW AND FOREVER, ONE AND INSEPARABLE."

SATURDAY, AUGUST 23, 1862.

A LETTER FROM THE PRESIDENT.

EXECUTIVE MANSION,
Washington, August 22, 1862.

Hon. HORACE GREELEY:

DEAR SIR: I have just read yours of the 19th, addressed to myself through the New York Tribune. If there be in it any statements, or assumptions of fact, which I may know to be erroneous, I do not now and here controvert them. If there be in it any inferences which I may believe to be falsely drawn, I do not now and here argue against them. If there be perceptible in it an impatient and dictatorial tone, I waive it in deference to an old friend whose heart I have always supposed to be right.

As to the policy I "seem to be pursuing," as you say, I have not meant to leave any one in doubt.

I would save the Union. I would save it the shortest way under the Constitution. The sooner the national authority can be restored the nearer the Union will be "the Union as it was." If there be those who would not save the Union unless they

On August 23, 1862, President Lincoln's response to Horace Greeley's criticism of his stance on slavery appeared in the *National Intelligencer*, a Washington, D.C., newspaper. In it, Lincoln said, "If I could save the Union without freeing any slave I would do it, and if I could save it by freeing all the slaves I would do it; and if I could save it by freeing some and leaving others alone I would also do that. What I do about slavery . . . I do because I believe it helps to save the Union."

September 17, 1862, Union and Confederate forces clashed near Sharpsburg, Maryland. The Union army forced the Confederate army to retreat and drove them from the North. This conflict was called the Battle of Antietam. It gave Lincoln the important victory he wanted. He began working on a final draft of the Emancipation Proclamation.

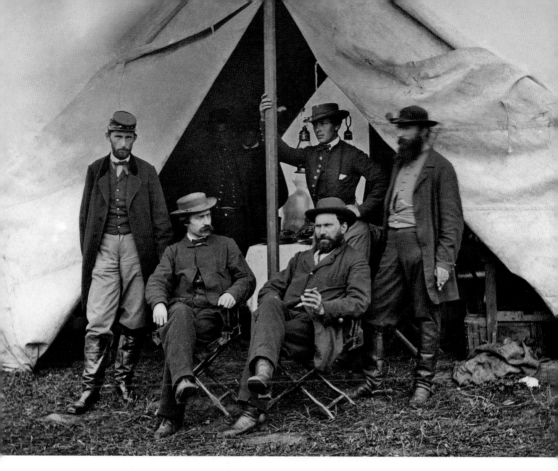

Alexander Gardner's photographs are a fascinating record of the events that took place at the Battle of Antietam.

A FIRSTHAND LOOK AT
THE BATTLE OF ANTIETAM

The Civil War was the first war in history to be widely photographed. Alexander Gardner was among the many photographers who produced firsthand images of the conflict. On September 19, 1862, he arrived at Sharpsburg, Maryland. It was two days after Union and Confederate troops clashed at Antietam Creek. More than 20,000 soldiers were killed or wounded. The battle was the bloodiest single day of fighting in U.S. history. See page 60 for a link to view Gardner's photographs online.

CHAPTER 3

THE PRELIMINARY PROCLAMATION

Lincoln's firsthand view of the Union victory at Antietam inspired him to issue the proclamation.

ABRAHAM LINCOLN CALLED his cabinet together once again on September 22, 1862. He announced that the Union's success at the Battle of Antietam provided an ideal moment for him to issue the Emancipation Proclamation.

Lincoln and his cabinet went over the proclamation one last time before issuing it.

The Draft Order

Lincoln read the order to his cabinet. It stated that all slaves in any state at war against the United States "shall be then, thenceforward, and forever free" after the new year began. The order called for emancipation of slaves in states that were in **rebellion** against the Union on January 1, 1863. Slaves would not be freed in states that were not fighting against the Union.

Lincoln based the order on the Confiscation Act. This act authorized the president to free runaway, captured, and abandoned slaves of rebel slave owners. He would issue a final order if the Confederate states did not return to the Union by January 1, 1863. That order would free their slaves. The order would not end slavery in the four border states because they were not in rebellion against the Union. This first order is now known as the **Preliminary** Emancipation Proclamation.

The Final Draft

Some cabinet members thought that the order would not be legal unless Congress passed a law that freed slaves. Lincoln disagreed. He asserted that he could issue the order under his authority as commander in chief of the U.S. forces. He argued that he was using his constitutional powers to conduct the war in order to restore the Union. Lincoln agreed to make several minor changes in language suggested by the cabinet members. He wrote out the final order after the meeting.

Slaves freed by the Confiscation Act were often referred to as "contrabands."

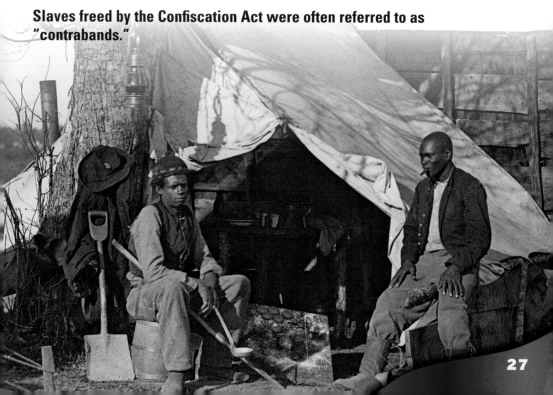

THE *FIRST READING OF THE* EMANCIPATION PROCLAMATION OF PRESIDENT LINCOLN

In February 1864, painter Francis Bicknell Carpenter convinced President Lincoln to let him create a painting to capture the historic moment when Lincoln discussed the Emancipation Proclamation with his cabinet. *First Reading of the Emancipation Proclamation of President Lincoln* was displayed in the East Room of the White House after its completion. Today, it hangs in the Capitol's west staircase in the Senate wing. See page 60 for a link to view the painting online.

Reaction in the North

Lincoln signed the Preliminary Emancipation Proclamation on September 22, 1862. The government quickly printed thousands of copies to distribute to government agencies, foreign officials, military commanders and troops, and newspapers.

Abolitionists and religious groups celebrated the release of the Preliminary Emancipation Proclamation. Governor David Tod of Ohio said that Lincoln "should be praised . . . for acting as President of South Carolina as well as Ohio." The Democratic governor of New York disagreed. He called the proclamation a "bloody, barbarous, revolutionary, and unconstitutional scheme." Some Union military commanders hoped that Lincoln's order would inspire their troops. Other officers quit their commissions and returned home. Many soldiers complained that they had not joined the army to free slaves.

Horace Greeley wrote, "It is the beginning of the end of the rebellion; the beginning of a new life for the nation." But some newspapers did not support the president's actions. An editorial in Connecticut's *Hartford Courant* called them unconstitutional.

Horace Greeley was a well-known journalist and political leader.

Reaction in the South

Most white Southerners believed the Preliminary Emancipation Proclamation would inspire slaves to leave the plantations in large numbers or rise up against slave owners. Several Southern states passed laws to help keep slaves from running away and from organizing uprisings.

YESTERDAY'S HEADLINES

On October 3, 1862, the Augusta, Georgia, *Chronicle & Sentinel* published an editorial about the Preliminary Emancipation Proclamation. It stated, "This document, this last desperate resort of the Federal Government [will] cause more trouble and dissatisfaction at the North than dismay at the South. . . . It will lose Lincoln many friends, and gain him none. . . . It will convince the wavering men of the border states that their only safety is under the Confederate banner."

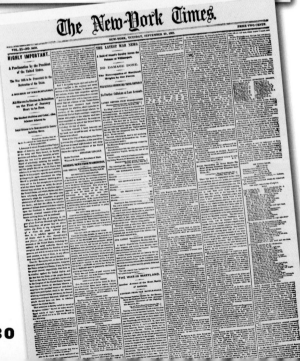

News of Lincoln's proclamation quickly reached slaves in the South. The proclamation was printed widely in Southern newspapers. Slaves who could read told other slaves about the order. The *New York Times* commented, "There is far more rapid and secret diffusing [spreading] of intelligence and news throughout the plantations than was ever dreamed of in the North."

One of Lincoln's goals in issuing the proclamation was to convince foreign countries to stop trading with the Confederacy. Southern politicians now worried that the order would harm the Confederacy's

The New York Times commented on how quickly news of emancipation spread through the South.

Lincoln hoped that the proclamation would damage the Southern economy by ruining trade relations with Great Britain and other foreign nations.

relationships with England and other nations. The South did not have enough factories to keep pace with the North's production of military supplies. The Confederates desperately needed to import weapons and other goods from overseas.

Reaction Abroad

Reaction to the Emancipation Proclamation in England was mixed. England had strong economic ties with the South. It imported large amounts of cotton, tobacco, and other raw materials. The U.S. **ambassador** to England reported that the proclamation had "strengthened feeling on both sides" of the issue. Lincoln's order put England in a difficult situation. The country had

A VIEW FROM ABROAD

On October 7, 1862, the *Times of London* published an editorial that strongly condemned the Preliminary Emancipation Proclamation. The editorial claimed that Lincoln wanted to set off slave riots in the South. It read, "He will appeal to the black blood of the African . . . and when the blood begins to flow and shrieks come piercing through the darkness, Mr. Lincoln will wait till the rising flames tell that all is consumed, and then he will rub his hands and think that revenge is sweet."

abolished slavery in 1833. But England had declared itself neutral at the beginning of the Civil War.

Powerful and influential people in England had reason to support the South. But the English government was reluctant to give diplomatic recognition and economic support to the South. They feared that the English public would riot to protest any official government support for a nation that maintained slavery.

Immediate Effects

The Emancipation Proclamation did not apply to Delaware, Maryland, Kentucky, or Missouri. But many slaves in these states simply ignored that fact. Some slaves in Maryland fled their owners and went to the District of Columbia. Slavery had been abolished there. Lincoln had gambled and won. The border states did not secede from the Union.

Slaves continued to be auctioned in border states such as Missouri, where the proclamation did not apply.

Several of Lincoln's cabinet members had warned him that issuing the Emancipation Proclamation would swing the 1862 elections against Republicans. Lincoln's opponents used the proclamation against Republicans running for office. Many voters were already upset about paying higher taxes to fund the war. They were also discouraged by the Union army's lack of success on the battlefield.

In the elections, Republicans lost 34 seats in the U.S. House of Representatives. But they still held on to their majorities in both the House and the Senate. The setback was not as serious as some Republicans had feared it would be. Democrats hoped the election results would force Lincoln to withdraw the Emancipation Proclamation. But he showed no sign of changing his mind.

CHAPTER 4

THE EMANCIPATION PROCLAMATION

Lincoln spent long hours revising and perfecting the proclamation.

THE EMANCIPATION PROCLAMATION

did not represent Lincoln's personal views on slavery. He wanted each state legislature to pass laws that freed slaves within its borders. He felt that the federal government should provide funds to compensate slave owners for the loss of their slaves. He intended the order to be a wartime measure only.

Lincoln discussed the final wording of the proclamation with Charles Sumner on Christmas Eve 1862. Sumner was a powerful Republican senator from Massachusetts. Lincoln and his cabinet discussed the Emancipation Proclamation for the last time on December 31. The president agreed to make a few minor changes to the order's wording. Then he began writing the final version.

Lincoln's signature made the proclamation official.

Lincoln Signs the Order

Lincoln hosted a New Year's Day party at the White House on January 1, 1863. He retired to his study after the party. Secretary of State Seward and a few other officials were waiting for him. The official Emancipation Proclamation order sat on Lincoln's desk awaiting his signature.

Before signing the order, Lincoln commented, "I never, in my life, felt more certain that I was doing right than I do in signing this paper." Copies of the Emancipation Proclamation were distributed to newspapers that evening. Government telegraph offices sent the text of the order to government and military officials.

The Order

The Emancipation Proclamation declared that "all persons held as slaves within any State, or designated part of a State, the people whereof shall then be in rebellion against the United States, shall be then, thenceforward, and forever free." Unlike the Preliminary Emancipation Proclamation, the final order provided no provision for compensating slave owners. The final order also authorized black men to

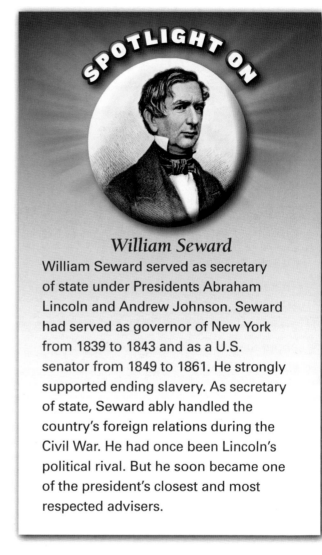

SPOTLIGHT ON

William Seward

William Seward served as secretary of state under Presidents Abraham Lincoln and Andrew Johnson. Seward had served as governor of New York from 1839 to 1843 and as a U.S. senator from 1849 to 1861. He strongly supported ending slavery. As secretary of state, Seward ably handled the country's foreign relations during the Civil War. He had once been Lincoln's political rival. But he soon became one of the president's closest and most respected advisers.

YESTERDAY'S HEADLINES

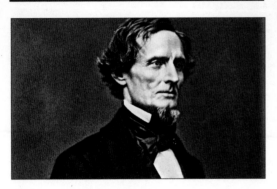

The January 31, 1863, edition of *Harper's Weekly* magazine reported Confederate president Jefferson Davis's comments about the Emancipation Proclamation. Davis said that the order encouraged slaves "to a general assassination" of their masters. He stated that although Southerners hated the proclamation, "the impotent [powerless] rage which it discloses" reassured them that the South would triumph in the war.

join the Union army.

Lincoln's order had no effect in Northern or border states or in sections of Confederate states that Union troops already occupied. Tennessee was mostly under the control of Union forces when the proclamation was issued, so the order did not apply to that state. It did apply to Alabama, Arkansas, Florida, Georgia, Mississippi, North Carolina, South Carolina, and Texas. It also applied to parts of Louisiana and Virginia.

Joy and Condemnation

African Americans filled Northern churches on the evening of December 31. They waited for the proclamation to go into effect at the stroke of midnight. Celebrations erupted throughout the North as word spread on January 1 that Lincoln had officially issued the Emancipation Proclamation. At an assembly to

The Emancipation Proclamation set the United States on the path toward ending slavery completely.

honor the proclamation in Boston, Frederick Douglass called it the "first step" in the emancipation of all slaves.

Many Southerners believed that the order would not change anything. One Virginian newspaper reporter wrote, "Wherever his [Lincoln's] armies have penetrated they have kidnapped every negro they could lay their hands on, and proclamation or no proclamation,

Southern slaves celebrated as news of the proclamation spread.

whenever they are able they will continue to do the same." Another Southern newspaper called the proclamation "the most startling political crime, and the most stupid political blunder, yet known in American history. . . . Southern people have now only to choose between victory and death."

Everyone knew that the order had freed slaves only in the parts of the South that the Union army controlled. Henry Ward Beecher proclaimed in a sermon that, "The Proclamation may not free a single slave, but it gives liberty a moral recognition." The Emancipation Proclamation made it clear that the federal government would no longer tolerate slavery in the Confederacy.

HON. ABRAHAM LINCOLN, OF ILLINOIS. FOR PRESIDENT.

HON. HANNIBAL HAMLIN, OF MAINE, FOR VICE PRESIDENT.

Lincoln wrote a letter to Vice President Hannibal Hamlin that communicated his doubts about the proclamation's potential effectiveness in the South.

A FIRSTHAND LOOK AT
LINCOLN'S LETTER TO HAMLIN

Abraham Lincoln wrote a letter to Vice President Hannibal Hamlin on September 28, 1862. The president described his feelings about the proclamation. He wrote, "While I hope something from the proclamation, my expectations are not as sanguine [hopeful] as are those of some friends. The time for its effect southward has not come; but northward the effect should be instantaneous." See page 60 for a link to view the contents of the letter online.

CHAPTER 5

AN IMMEDIATE IMPACT

After the Emancipation Proclamation, Union soldiers freed slaves as they made their way through Southern states.

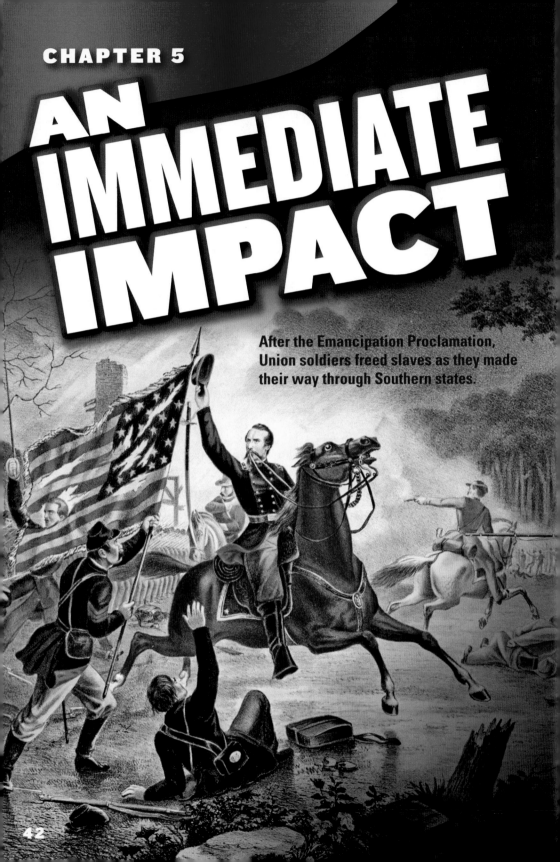

THE EMANCIPATION PROCLAMATION applied to 10 Confederate states. The U.S. government could not enforce Lincoln's order in those states until the Union army gained control of some territory in a state. But the impact of Lincoln's order changed the focus of the war. The conflict was no longer just about preserving and restoring the Union. It was now also about ending slavery.

Many slaves made their way north after being freed by Union soldiers.

Seizing Freedom

Slaves in the northern and western parts of the Confederacy left their owners in significant numbers after the Emancipation Proclamation became official on January 1, 1863. Many made their way to Union military posts in the South. Others ran away to one of the Union states. Some slaves in the Deep South stayed with their masters. Some remained because it was the only life they knew. Others stayed because they feared being punished for running away. Many slaves throughout the South refused to work. They preferred to wait for Union troops to liberate them.

A FIRSTHAND LOOK AT
A SLAVE'S EMANCIPATION

African American leader Booker T. Washington wrote about his emancipation in *Up from Slavery: An Autobiography*. Shortly after the war ended, a Union officer arrived at the plantation where nine-year-old Booker lived. The officer read the Emancipation Proclamation to the gathered slaves. Washington wrote, "We were told that we were all free, and could go when and where we pleased. My mother . . . leaned over and kissed her children, while tears of joy ran down her cheeks. She explained . . . this was the day for which she had been so long praying, but fearing that she would never live to see." See page 60 for a link to read this book.

The Union army freed local slaves as it advanced through the South. Masses of former slaves overwhelmed Union military posts in both the North and the South. Soldiers set up temporary tent cities and cared for the newly freed people. Many former slaves worked for the Union army. They cooked, washed clothes, and performed manual labor.

Black Recruitment

The Emancipation Proclamation allowed black men to become soldiers in the Union army. It asked former slaves to join "the armed services of the United States to garrison forts, positions, stations, and other places, and to man vessels of all sorts." The War Department created the Bureau of Colored Troops to oversee the **recruitment** and training of black soldiers. Nearly 200,000 black men had volunteered to serve in the Union army by the end of the war. About three-quarters of them were former slaves.

Many freed slaves joined the Union army and helped free other slaves.

Military leaders on both sides recognized that a huge surge in Union troop numbers could shift the war decisively in the North's favor. Confederate president Jefferson Davis announced that Union officers who commanded black troops would be executed if they were captured. Black soldiers who were captured would be sold into slavery. Lincoln answered by promising that a Confederate officer would be executed for each Union officer executed by the Confederates.

Some blacks did not join the Union army. They could find jobs that paid well in factories without risking their lives or being captured and sold as slaves. And some white soldiers mistreated black recruits. White officers often gave black soldiers the worst assignments. These assignments usually involved heavy labor. Black soldiers were paid $10 a month. White soldiers received $16.50. The pay for both was made equal by the end of the war.

The Confederacy Weakens

The loss of slaves drained the Confederacy's ability to wage the war. Slave labor was a key part of the South's war machine. Slaves produced cotton crops that financed the purchase of weapons and other military supplies. They built roads, forts, and railways. They also labored in factories, shipyards, and hospitals.

The Confederacy also experienced political and military troubles. The Confederate states were slow to provide funds to their central government to finance

SPOTLIGHT ON

The 54th Massachusetts Regiment

The 54th Massachusetts Regiment was the Union's first black regiment. It was chosen to lead the July 18, 1863, attack on Fort Wagner near Charleston, South Carolina. The regiment's white commander was named Colonel Robert G. Shaw. He told his men, "I want you to prove yourselves. The eyes of thousands will look on what you do tonight."

Many of the men were killed as they stormed the fort in an unsuccessful attempt to overtake it. But their bravery won them great respect and led to an increase in Union recruitment of African Americans.

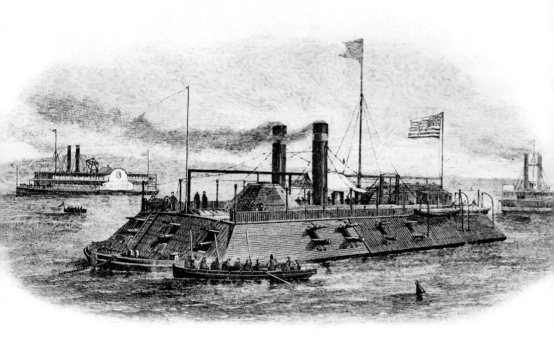

The Union blockade prevented supply ships from entering or leaving Southern ports.

the war. The high number of battle casualties also took a toll on the Confederate army. Soldiers began to leave the army in significant numbers. A blockade by the Union navy greatly reduced the shipment of crops from Southern ports. It also reduced the ability of the military to import supplies. Major Union victories at Gettysburg, Pennsylvania, and Vicksburg, Mississippi, appeared to have turned the tide of the war by the summer of 1863.

The Union army wore down Confederate forces throughout 1864. General Ulysses S. Grant led 120,000 Union soldiers in an advance toward the Confederate capital at Richmond, Virginia. Confederate general

Robert E. Lee had only 64,000 men to stop them. Union general William T. Sherman commanded more than 100,000 men in the West against Confederate general Joseph E. Johnston's 60,000-man force.

The War Ends

Voters in the Union cast their ballots for president on November 8, 1864. Lincoln won the election in a landslide. He beat Democratic candidate George McClellan. McClellan was the former commanding general of the Union army.

Lincoln gave his second inaugural address in March 1865. He promised to reunite the country "with malice [hatred] toward none; with charity for all." He encouraged Northerners and Southerners "to do all which may achieve and cherish a just and lasting peace, among ourselves, and with all nations."

The Confederacy was near its end by the spring of 1865. Union troops entered Richmond on April 4. Jefferson Davis and other Confederate leaders fled south. Five days later, Lee surrendered to Grant at Appomattox, Virginia. The war was almost over.

Free at Last

The Emancipation Proclamation did not abolish slavery in the United States. It did not guarantee slaves their freedom after the war ended. Nor did the Union have a law to prevent a state from legalizing slavery within its borders. Abolitionists wanted Congress to pass a law

Celebration broke out in the House of Representatives as the 13th Amendment was passed.

that would forever eliminate slavery in the United States.

Congress approved the 13th Amendment to the U.S. Constitution in January 1865. It abolished slavery in the United States. Lincoln approved the amendment. It was then sent to the individual state legislatures for consideration. The Constitution requires that three-quarters of the states **ratify** a proposed amendment before it becomes law.

Lincoln did not live to see the amendment passed. On April 14, 1865, John Wilkes Booth shot the president at a performance of the play *Our American Cousin* in Washington, D.C. Booth was an actor who supported the Confederacy. He hoped that Lincoln's death would strengthen the Confederacy. Lincoln died the next morning. Vice President Andrew Johnson was sworn in as president. He promised to continue many of Lincoln's policies. This included supporting ratification of the 13th Amendment.

The authors of *The Emancipation Proclamation: Three Views*, published in 2006, offer three different modern views of the Emancipation Proclamation. Edna Greene Medford claims that the proclamation "fortified black people in their struggle" but accomplished little else. Frank J. Williams writes that the proclamation "was greater than the sum of its parts" and should be "remembered as a great document." Harold Holzer believes that *First Reading of the Emancipation Proclamation of President Lincoln* and other art helped establish Lincoln as the Great Emancipator after his death.

It took almost one year for that to happen. On December 6, 1865, Secretary of State William Seward announced that three-quarters of the states had ratified the 13th Amendment. Slavery was now illegal throughout the United States. The remaining slaves in the country were free at last.

What Happened Where?

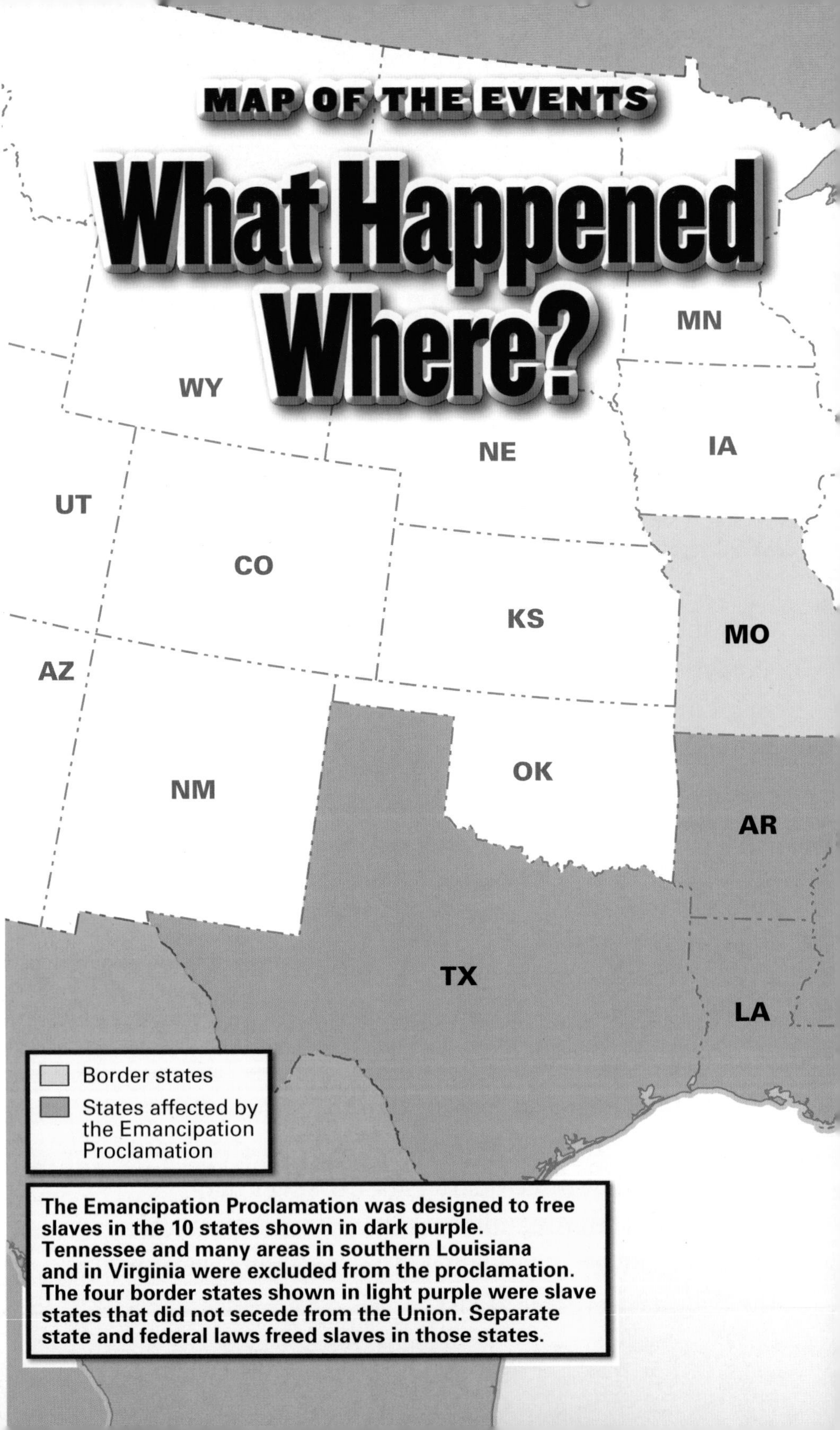

MN

WY

NE

IA

UT

CO

KS

MO

AZ

NM

OK

AR

TX

LA

Border states

States affected by the Emancipation Proclamation

The Emancipation Proclamation was designed to free slaves in the 10 states shown in dark purple. Tennessee and many areas in southern Louisiana and in Virginia were excluded from the proclamation. The four border states shown in light purple were slave states that did not secede from the Union. Separate state and federal laws freed slaves in those states.

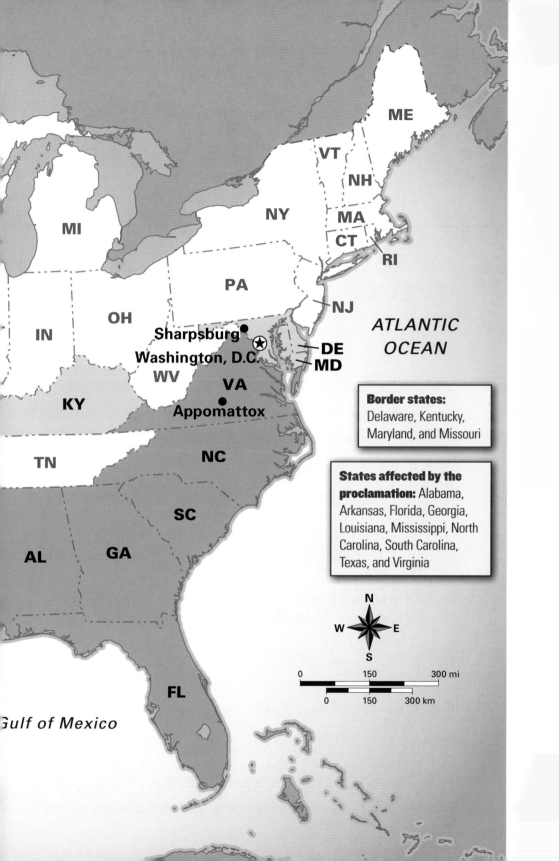

ME

VT

NH

NY

MA

CT

RI

MI

PA

NJ

ATLANTIC OCEAN

OH

IN

Sharpsburg

Washington, D.C.

DE

MD

WV

VA

KY

Appomattox

TN

NC

Border states:
Delaware, Kentucky, Maryland, and Missouri

SC

States affected by the proclamation: Alabama, Arkansas, Florida, Georgia, Louisiana, Mississippi, North Carolina, South Carolina, Texas, and Virginia

AL

GA

N

W — E

S

0   150   300 mi

0   150   300 km

FL

Gulf of Mexico

Groundwork for Equality

Because of Lincoln's leadership during the Civil War, many people consider him one of the greatest presidents in U.S. history.

After the surrender of the Confederacy, the federal government passed laws and adopted policies to reunite the country and rebuild the South. Two constitutional amendments were ratified to protect the civil rights of former slaves. The 14th Amendment guaranteed due process and equal protection of the law to all citizens. The 15th Amendment guaranteed the right to vote to African American men.

But southern state and local governments had passed laws by the late 1870s that greatly limited the rights of African Americans. These laws created a **segregated** society. They also made it difficult for African Americans to vote. Whites and blacks went to separate public schools. They ate in separate restaurants and traveled in separate train cars. African Americans in the South became second-class citizens.

African Americans fought a long, hard battle to secure equal rights. The U.S. Supreme Court ruled in 1954 that state laws establishing separate public schools for black and white students were unconstitutional. Later Supreme Court cases struck down other segregation laws. The civil rights movement of the 1950s and 1960s helped secure equal rights and treatment for black citizens.

This slow movement started 150 years ago. It was the Emancipation Proclamation that laid the groundwork for the vast changes that led to greater equality and freedom for people in America.

INFLUENTIAL INDIVIDUALS

William H. Seward

William H. Seward (1801–1872) served as secretary of state in the Lincoln and Johnson administrations. He was one of Lincoln's closest advisers.

Gideon Welles (1802–1878) served as secretary of the navy during the Lincoln and Johnson administrations. He was one of Lincoln's closest advisers.

David Hunter (1802–1886) was a general in the Union army. Lincoln canceled Hunter's 1862 military order freeing slaves in South Carolina, Georgia, and Florida.

Robert E. Lee (1807–1870) commanded the Confederate Army of Northern Virginia and was named general in chief of the Confederate armies less than three months before the war ended.

Salmon Chase (1808–1873) served as secretary of the treasury and as chief justice of the U.S. Supreme Court during the Civil War. He strongly supported the abolition of slavery.

Andrew Johnson (1808–1875) served as vice president during Lincoln's second term. He became president when Lincoln was assassinated in April 1865.

Jefferson Davis

Jefferson Davis (1808–1889) was president of the Confederate States of America. He believed that the Emancipation Proclamation would have little impact on the war.

Abraham Lincoln (1809–1865) served as the 16th U.S. president. He issued the Emancipation Proclamation on January 1, 1863. It was the first major step toward the abolition of slavery in the United States.

Hannibal Hamlin (1809–1891) served as vice president during Lincoln's first term. He was the first person to see Lincoln's first draft of the Emancipation Proclamation.

Horace Greeley (1811–1872) was the influential editor of the *New York Tribune*. A strong abolitionist, he criticized Lincoln's cautious approach to ending slavery.

Charles Sumner (1811–1874) was an influential abolitionist senator from Massachusetts.

Montgomery Blair (1813–1883) served as postmaster general in the Lincoln administration. As a cabinet member, he warned Lincoln about the possible political consequences of issuing the Emancipation Proclamation.

Henry Ward Beecher (1813–1887) was a minister. One of the nation's leading abolitionists, he criticized Lincoln for not declaring the abolition of slavery a goal of the Civil War.

Frederick Douglass (1817–1895) was the leading black abolitionist before and during the Civil War. A former slave, he criticized Lincoln's inaction on slavery.

Frederick Douglass

Ulysses S. Grant (1822–1885) was appointed as the chief general of the Union army in 1864. He pushed his forces south, capturing Richmond in April 1865 and accepting Lee's surrender that same month.

George McClellan (1826–1885) was the chief general of the Union army until 1863. The Democratic candidate for president in 1864, he lost to Lincoln.

Booker T. Washington (1856–1915) was born into slavery in Virginia. He became a noted educator and an influential speaker on African American issues.

TIMELINE

1619	1860	1861	1862

1619
The first African slaves arrive in what is now the United States.

1860
November 6
Abraham Lincoln is elected president.

1861
March 4
President Lincoln is inaugurated.

April 12
The American Civil War begins.

August 6
Congress passes the Confiscation Act, allowing the military to take in runaway slaves.

1862
April 16
Lincoln signs a bill freeing all slaves in the District of Columbia.

June 19
Lincoln signs legislation abolishing slavery in the western territories.

July 22
Lincoln discusses the Emancipation Proclamation with his cabinet.

September 17
The Confederates retreat after the Battle of Antietam.

September 22
President Lincoln reads the Preliminary Emancipation Proclamation to his cabinet.

1863

January 1
President Lincoln signs the Emancipation Proclamation.

July 1–3
The Union Army wins the Battle of Gettysburg.

July 18
The 54th Massachusetts Regiment fights at Fort Wagner, South Carolina.

1864

September 1
Union general William Sherman captures Atlanta, Georgia.

November 8
Lincoln is reelected president.

1865

January
Congress approves the 13th Amendment.

March 4
Lincoln is inaugurated for his second term.

April 4
Union forces capture Richmond, Virginia, the capital of the Confederacy.

April 9
Confederate general Robert E. Lee surrenders at Appomattox Court House, Virginia, ending the Civil War.

April 14
Lincoln is shot by John Wilkes Booth.

April 15
Lincoln dies; Vice President Andrew Johnson is sworn in as president.

December 6
The 13th Amendment is ratified, permanently abolishing slavery in the United States.

LIVING HISTORY

Primary sources provide firsthand evidence about a topic. Witnesses to a historical event create primary sources. They include autobiographies, newspaper reports of the time, oral histories, photographs, and memoirs. A secondary source analyzes primary sources, and is one step or more removed from the event. Secondary sources include textbooks, encyclopedias, and commentaries.

Booker T. Washington's Autobiography To read Booker T. Washington's autobiography *Up from Slavery* go to *http://xroads .virginia.edu/~HYPER/washington/cover.html*

The District of Columbia Emancipation Act To view the District of Columbia Emancipation Act go to *www.archives.gov /exhibits/featured_documents/dc_emancipation_act*

First Reading of the Emancipation Proclamation of President Lincoln To view Francis Bicknell Carpenter's painting of Lincoln and his cabinet discussing the Emancipation Proclamation, visit *www.senate.gov/artandhistory/art/artifact/Painting_33_00005.htm*

Photos from the Battle of Antietam To see an assortment of photographs taken by Alexander Gardner at the battlefield at Antietam, go to *www.nps.gov/ancm/photosmultimedia/index.htm*

A President at Work To read Major Thomas T. Eckert's account of President Lincoln at work on the Emancipation Proclamation go to *www.mrlincolnswhitehouse.org/inside.asp?ID=630&subjectID=4*

President Lincoln's Letter to Vice President Hannibal Hamlin To read Lincoln's letter to his vice president, visit *http:// teachingamericanhistory.org/library/index.asp?document=416*

President Lincoln's Response to General Order No. 11 To see Lincoln's handwritten reversal of General Order No. 11, go to *http://memory.loc.gov/cgi-bin/ampage?collId=mal&fileName=mal1 /160/1604600/malpage.db&recNum=0*